The Gift of Love

'Enfolded in Love' series
General Editor: Robert Llewelyn

THE GIFT OF LOVE

Daily Readings with
John Wesley

Introduced and edited by
Arthur Skevington Wood

Darton, Longman and Todd
London

First published in 1987 by
Darton, Longman and Todd Ltd
89 Lillie Road, London SW6 1UD

Introduction and arrangement
© 1987 Arthur Skevington Wood

ISBN 0 232 51699 5

British Library Cataloguing in Publication Data

Wesley, John
  The gift of love: daily readings with
John Wesley.—("Enfolded in love" series)
1. Devotional calendars
I. Title II. Wood, Arthur Skevington
III. Series
242'.2   BV48.10

ISBN 0–232–51699–5

Phototypeset by
Input Typesetting Ltd, London SW19 8DR
Printed and bound in Great Britain by
Anchor Brendon Ltd, Tiptree, Essex

Contents

John Wesley's spiritual pilgrimage

John Wesley fulfilled more than one role on the stage of eighteenth-century life. First and foremost, however, he was an itinerant evangelist. As he himself explained, he was called by God 'to spread scriptural holiness over the land'. In a ministry stretching over more than fifty years, he travelled the length and breadth of Britain, usually on horseback, in order to 'offer Christ'. He spent most of his days in the saddle as a gospel outrider and must have covered over a quarter of a million miles in all. His stated aim was 'not to form any new sect; but to reform the nation, particularly the Church'.

Wesley was a born leader and organizer. He saw the need to conserve the gains of mission by gathering his converts into classes for the purpose of spiritual nurture and growth. These in turn were linked together in local societies along lines already familiar at the time. The united societies which he supervised were seen by him as embraced within the Church of England, although attracting the name of Methodist. Wesley never took a living, but regarded the world as his parish. He remained in Anglican orders to the end.

He acted as a father-in-God to a nationwide circle of believers. His correspondence reflects both the range of his influence and the effectiveness of his pastoral counselling. His now classic Journal provides a day-to-day account of his missionary journeys as well as a fascinating commentary on contemporary conditions. His published works, running to fourteen volumes, include sermons, tracts and more substantial treatises. He is nowadays increasingly recognized as a folk theologian: he himself declared that he designed 'plain truth for plain people'. His prose style may on occasion strike strangely on modern ears but, compared with the elaborate literary arabesques composed by many of his contemporaries, Wesley's writings are direct and lucid. His classical education gave him a feel for words and his training in logic ensured that his thoughts were always well marshalled.

THE RECTORY, EPWORTH, LINCOLNSHIRE
Credit: The Mansell Collection

John Wesley was born at Epworth, Lincolnshire, on 17 June 1703. His father, Samuel, was rector of the parish, though he, like his wife Susannah, had been brought up as a nonconformist. This dual strain is apparent in Wesley: he was indebted at once to the catholic, reformed and puritan traditions. As a boy he was the last of the family to be rescued from a disastrous fire which destroyed the Epworth rectory. He would later refer to himself as 'a brand plucked out of the burning' (Amos 4:11) and was convinced that his life had been spared by the providence of God in order that he might fulfil a special vocation.

It was not until he was twenty-two years of age and up at Oxford that Wesley began to be seriously concerned about his spiritual condition. God often approaches us along the line of our own interests. Wesley was a scholar and an avid reader. It was through three books in particular that he was guided in his quest for holiness. One was Thomas à Kempis's *The Imitation of Christ*, or *The Christian Pattern* as Wesley calls it. It was now that he 'began to see that true religion was seated in the heart, and that God's law extended to all our thoughts as well as words and actions'. He considered à Kempis rather strict, but nevertheless tells us that he 'began to aim at, and pray for, inward holiness'. He corresponded with his godly mother about what he had read.

Wesley was also impressed by Jeremy Taylor's *Holy Living and Holy Dying*. He felt that what he discovered in it about humility and a repentant spirit was especially relevant to his situation. It was at this stage that Wesley started to live by rule. His diary (as distinct from the Journal) was set out very much according to the plan suggested by Bishop Taylor. Three groups of rules and resolutions are placed as a kind of preface. There is a general rule covering all actions in life, followed by further rules for the employment of time and for achieving purity of intention.

A third book to influence Wesley was William Law's *A Serious Call to a Devout and Holy Life*, together with his lesser-known treatise on Christian perfection. These 'convinced me more than ever', Wesley testified, 'of the absolute impossibility of being half a Christian'. He thereupon determined, by the strength of grace, 'to be all devoted to God, – to give him all my soul, my body, and my substance'. He declared that, as a consequence, 'the light flowed in so mightily upon my soul that everything appeared in a new view'.

But what Wesley added in the next sentence is revealing. 'And by my continued endeavour to keep his whole law, inward and outward, to the utmost of my power, I was persuaded that I should be accepted of him, and that I was even then in a state of salvation.' On the one hand it is clear that here was a significant step forward in Wesley's Christian pilgrimage. The need for total commitment was brought into focus and from this point onwards he prepared himself for ordination. On the other hand, however, he was still only a seeker after holiness. He now saw the goal but did not yet know how it might be attained. He was to learn that there can be no holiness without a deep personal relationship with Christ as the risen Redeemer, and that this is only made possible by grace through faith.

John Wesley left Oxford temporarily on two occasions to assist his father at Epworth and at nearby Wroot. Meanwhile he had been elected fellow of Lincoln College and seemed to be settling for an academic career. When he returned to the University after the second absence, he found that his brother Charles had gathered together a few like-minded friends to form what became known as the Holy Club. John soon assumed the leadership and began to change its shape somewhat, so that its original semi-educational aim gave place to that of concentrated spiritual improvement and practical Christian service in relieving the poor and disadvantaged.

Wesley was before long to exchange the religion of a hermit for that of a frontiersman, as an American writer has phrased it. In 1735 he and Charles went off to the colony of Georgia with high hopes of missionary success among the Indians. Wesley's self-analysis affords an instructive glimpse into his spiritual condition. 'My chief motive . . . is the hope of saving my own soul. I hope to learn the true sense of the gospel by preaching it to the heathen.' He came back disappointed and disillusioned. 'I went to America to convert the Indians,' he declared, 'but, oh, who shall convert me? . . . I have a fair summer religion. I can talk well, . . . but let death look me in the face, and my spirit is troubled.' That fear of dying had been accentuated first by a severe illness not long before he left Georgia, and then by a terrifying storm at sea on the return voyage. A couplet from one of John Donne's sonnets haunted him:

I have a sin of fear that, when I've spun
My last thread, I shall perish on the shore.

It was through this harrowing experience of

despair that Wesley was led to realize that what he lacked was a vital faith to bring him lasting assurance. He explains that what he sought was the faith of a son rather than that of a servant. 'The faith I want is "a sure trust and confidence in God, that, through the merits of Christ, my sins are forgiven, and I am reconciled to the favour of God".' It was largely through the wise counselling of a Moravian, Peter Boehler, that Wesley was eventually brought to know in his heart what he had already grasped with his mind. It was, moreover, as Dr Albert C. Outler neatly expresses it, 'a change from faith in faith to faith itself.

'I was now thoroughly convinced,' Wesley admitted; 'and, by the grace of God, I resolved to seek it unto the end, (1) by absolutely renouncing all dependence, in whole or in part, upon *my own* works of righteousness; on which I had really founded my hope of salvation, though I knew it not, from my youth up; (2) by adding to the constant use of all the other means of grace, continued prayer for this very thing, justifying, saving faith, a full reliance on the blood of Christ shed for *me*; a trust in him, as *my* Christ, as *my* sole justification, sanctification and redemption.' Wesley's own emphasis indicates the personal nature of the experience for which he yearned. It came to him on 24 May 1738. At a little meeting in Aldersgate Street, London, someone was reading from Luther's preface to Romans. This is what Wesley heard: 'So let us conclude that faith alone justifies, and alone fulfils the law. For faith indeed, through the merit of Christ, obtains the Holy Spirit, and the Spirit makes our heart new –

exhilarates, excites and inflames it, so that it may willingly do those things which the law commands.' And here is Wesley's well-known testimony: 'About a quarter before nine, while he was describing the change which God works in the heart through faith in Christ, I felt my heart strangely warmed. I felt I did trust in Christ, Christ alone, for salvation; and an assurance was given me that he had taken away my sins, even *mine*, and saved *me* from the law of sin and death.'

So, as Professor George Croft Cell put it, Wesley 'crossed his religious Rubicon'. The Aldersgate experience proved to be the turning point of his ministry. It launched him on what was to develop into a nationwide mission. He had now received the witness of the Spirit to confirm that he was made right with God by grace through faith. From this time forward the message of justification was to be his standing topic, to use his own expression, as he preached to the unconverted. The conviction that had burned its way into his own soul was to drive him out into the highways and byways of Britain to declare the good news of salvation for all.

Visitors can see the striking memorial outside the new Museum of London built on the site of Wesley's heart-warming. The design of the monument, which stands twenty feet high, symbolizes the wind and fire of the Holy Spirit. It records the events of the determinative day in 1738 as set out in Wesley's own Journal. Since its dedication in 1981 it has become a place of pilgrimage for Christians from all over the world, who thank

God for the transformation which resulted from Wesley's initiative in evangelism.

For over fifty years, until his death in 1791, Wesley was engaged in tireless activity directed towards the spread of the Christian gospel. He was fond of repeating a prayer of Nicholas Stratford, Bishop of Chester: 'Lord, let me not live to be useless!' From now on, his single-minded objective was to offer Christ to the masses of the people. He did so mainly through the medium of open-air preaching. At first he was reluctant to make such a venture, but he soon recognized its effectiveness and employed it as the spearhead of his strategy. The fields, the market places, the parks, the hillsides, the pitheads provided him with a pulpit. His brother Charles – the prolific hymn-writer – was his comrade-in-arms in this spiritual battle of Britain, as was his Oxford friend, George Whitefield, despite a difference in theological outlook. Soon a team of helpers, both clerical and lay, joined him in the fight and the campaign was intensified to cover the land.

Wesley himself travelled incessantly to keep in touch with his assistants and to meet with the converts. He shared the rigours of active service as he faced the hazards of storm and flood as well as, on occasion, the violence of the mob. The records present an appealingly human picture of Wesley in his endurance of hardship and his warm relationship with his fellow-workers.

It must not be imagined, however, that he was so consumed by evangelistic zeal as to be indifferent to the social and economic needs of the people to whom he ministered. That was far from the case. He had a profound concern for the plight of the poor. When the *Gentleman's Magazine* reported his death, the feature of his achievement singled out for special commendation was his doing 'infinite good to the lower classes'. Wesley made sure that offerings for the poor were regularly taken up in his societies. Schemes of work were devised for the unemployed; a lending stock was set up to fund those who were hoping to start a business of their own; the Strangers' Friend Societies backed by Wesley were designed to provide relief for the poor.

Wesley's own life-style was simple in the extreme. 'If I leave behind me ten pounds,' he wrote, 'you and all mankind bear witness against me, that I lived and died a thief and a robber.' In 1776 he received a letter from the Commissioners of Excise suggesting that he had failed to submit a return for tax purposes. They alleged that he possessed plate which he had not reported to them. Wesley's reply was brief and significant. 'I have two silver spoons at London and two at Bristol. This is all the plate which I have at present; and I shall not buy any more while so many round me want bread.'

Poverty was by no means the only social evil Wesley endeavoured to counteract. He was one of the first to lift up his voice against the slave trade in British colonies. As early as 1774 he published his *Thoughts on Slavery* in which he expressed himself in unambiguous terms. Four days before his death Wesley wrote to William Wilberforce, urging him on in his abolitionist crusade. 'Unless the divine power has raised you up to be as *Athan-*

THE AGED WESLEY WRITES AGAINST SLAVERY
Credit: Mary Evans Picture Library

asius contra mundum, I see not how you can go through your glorious enterprise in opposing that execrable villainy, which is the scandal of religion, of England, and of human nature. . . But if God be for you, who can be against you? Are all of them together stronger than God? O be not weary in well doing! Go on, in the name of God, and in the power of his might, till even American slavery (the vilest that ever saw the sun) shall vanish away before it.'

Long before John Howard appeared on the scene, Wesley had sought to arouse the national conscience to realize the urgent need for prison reform. Wesley regarded Howard as 'one of the greatest men in Europe' and Howard in turn was quick to acknowledge his debt to Wesley. 'I was encouraged by him to go on vigorously with my own designs. I saw in him how much a single man might achieve by zeal and perseverance.' Wesley's denunciation of war was as trenchant as his attacks on slavery and prison conditions. In his treatise on original sin he referred to it as 'a horrid reproach to the Christian name, yea, to the name of man'. 'Who can reconcile war', he asked, 'I will not say to religion, but to any degree of reason or common sense?'

If Wesley's experience of the warmed heart was determinative for his evangelistic and social mission, as we have seen, it was equally crucial for his understanding of holiness. Faith in what Christ had done *for* him brought the assurance of salvation. Faith in what Christ would do *in* him pointed the way of sanctification. Henceforward scriptural holiness was Wesley's major theme as he sought to instruct those who had been led to Christ. He constantly exhorted them not to stand still in the Christian life but to press on to maturity. This is what he aimed to do himself and this is what he expected from his people. He spoke variously in terms of full salvation, Christian perfection, or entire sanctification. But he preferred above all to treat holiness as perfect love – 'love excluding sin'. Here lies Wesley's distinctive contribution both to theology and to spirituality.

As Professor Albert C. Outler has shown, Wesley was impressed by the Byzantine teaching associated with Gregory of Nyssa and his own Anglican tradition as reflected in the writings of John Jewel, Joseph Hall and Jeremy Taylor. The ancient and Eastern emphasis on holiness as *disciplined* love was fused in Wesley's mind with the Anglican emphasis on holiness as *aspiring* love. This insight lies behind his unremitting insistence on the necessity of sanctification for the growth not only of the individual believer but of the Church as a whole. Wesley used the criterion of holiness to measure the progress of his societies. Without it, he claimed, 'be the preachers never so eloquent, there is little increase, either in the number or grace of the hearers'. The extracts collected in this book reflect Wesley's preoccupation with the quest for scriptural holiness. It is to be hoped that they will prompt those who read them to 'aim at . . . a holy life, for without that no one will see the Lord' (Hebrews 12:14, New English Bible).

ARTHUR SKEVINGTON WOOD

WESLEY'S CHAPEL, CITY ROAD, LONDON
OPENED 1778
Credit: The Mansell Collection

Knowing God

What a miserable drudgery is the service of God, unless I love the God whom I serve! But I cannot love one whom I know not. How then can I love God till I know him? And how is it possible I should know God, unless he make himself known unto me?

The whole creation speaks that there is a God. But who will show me what that God is? The more I reflect, the more convinced I am, that it is not possible for any or all the creatures to take off the veil which is on my heart, that I might discern this unknown God; to draw the curtain back which now hangs between, that I may see him who is invisible.

This veil of flesh now hides him from my sight; and who is able to make it transparent so that I may perceive, through this glass, God always before me, till I see him 'face to face'?

O my friend, how will you get one step farther, unless God reveal himself to your soul? And why should this seem a thing incredible to you that God, a Spirit, and the Father of the spirits of all flesh, should discover himself to your spirit?

Desire nothing but God

Beware of desiring anything but God. Now you desire nothing else; every other desire is driven out; see that none enter again. 'Keep thyself pure'; let your 'eye' remain 'single, and your whole body shall be full of light'. Admit no desire of pleasing food, or any other pleasures of sense; no desire of pleasing the eye or the imagination by anything grand, or new, or beautiful; no desire of money, of praise, or esteem; of happiness in any creature. You may bring these desires back, but you need not; you need feel them no more. O stand fast in the liberty wherewith Christ hath made you free!

Be patterns to all of denying yourselves and taking up your cross daily. Let them see that you make no account of any pleasure which does not bring you nearer to God, nor regard any pain which does; that you simply aim at pleasing him, whether by doing or suffering; that the constant language of your heart, with regard to pleasure or pain, honour or dishonour, riches or poverty, is

'All's alike to me, so I
In my Lord may live and die.'

Self-knowledge

By the grace of God, know thyself. Know and feel that thou wast shapen in wickedness and in sin did thy mother conceive thee; and that thou thyself hast been heaping sin upon sin, ever since thou couldst discern good from evil. Own thyself guilty of eternal death, and renounce all hope of ever being able to save thyself.

Be it all thy hope, to be washed in his blood and purified by his Spirit, 'who himself bore' all 'thy sins in his own body on the tree'. And if thou knowest he hath taken away thy sins, so much the more abase thyself before him in a continual sense of thy total dependence on him for every good thought, and word, and work, and of thy utter inability to all good unless he 'water thee every moment'.

Real Christianity

Beware, then, thou who art called by the name of Christ that thou come not short of the mark of thy high calling. Beware thou rest not, either in a natural state, with too many that are accounted *good Christians*; or in a legal state, wherein those who are highly esteemed of men are generally content to live and die.

Nay, but God hath prepared better things for thee, if thou follow on till thou attain. Thou art not called to fear and tremble, like devils; but to rejoice and love, like the angels of God.

Thou shalt do the will of God on earth as it is done in heaven. O prove thou 'what is that good, and acceptable, and perfect will of God'! Now present thyself 'a living sacrifice, holy, acceptable to God'. 'Whereunto thou hast already attained, hold fast', by 'reaching forth unto those things which are before'; until 'the God of peace make thee perfect in every good work, working in thee that which is well-pleasing in his sight, through Jesus Christ: to whom be glory for ever and ever, Amen.'

Scriptural religion

What is religion – I mean scriptural religion, for all other is the vainest of vain dreams; what is the very root of this religion? It is Immanuel, God with us. God in man! Heaven connected with earth! The unspeakable union of mortal with immortal. For 'truly our fellowship' (may all Christians say) 'is with the Father, and with his Son Jesus Christ. God hath given unto us eternal life, and this life is in his Son.'

How admirably does this life of God branch out into the whole of religion – I mean scriptural religion! As soon as God reveals his Son in the heart of a sinner, he is enabled to say, 'The life I now live, I live by faith in the Son of God, who loved me and gave himself for me.'

He then 'rejoices in hope of the glory of God', even with joy unspeakable. And in consequence both of this faith and hope, the love of God is shed abroad in his heart, which, filling the soul with love to all mankind, 'is the fulfilling of the law'.

And how wonderfully do both faith and love connect God with man and time with eternity!

New life in Christ

While a man is in a mere natural state before he is born of God he has, in a spiritual sense, eyes and sees not: a thick, impenetrable veil lies upon them. He has ears, but hears not: he is utterly deaf to what he is most of all concerned to hear. His other spiritual senses are all locked up: he is in the same condition as if he had them not.

Hence he has no knowledge of God, no intercourse with him. He is not at all acquainted with him. He has no true knowledge of the things of God, either of spiritual or eternal things. Therefore, though he is a living man, he is a dead Christian.

But as soon as he is born of God, there is a total change in all these particulars. Now he may be properly said to live. God having quickened him by his Spirit, he is alive to God through Jesus Christ. He lives a life which the world knoweth not of, a 'life which is hid with Christ in God'.

Our need of Christ

In every state we need Christ in the following respects: (1) Whatever grace we receive, it is a free gift from him. (2) We receive it as his purchase, merely in consideration of the price he paid. (3) We have this grace, not only from Christ, but in him. For our perfection is not like that of a tree, which flourishes by the sap derived from its own root, but like that of a branch, which, united to the vine, bears fruit, but severed from it is dried up and withered.

(4) All our blessings, temporal, spiritual and eternal, depend on his intercession for us, which is one branch of his priestly office, whereof therefore we have always equal need.

(5) The best of men still need Christ in his priestly office, to atone for their omissions, their short-comings, their mistakes in judgement and practice, and their defects of various kinds. For these are all deviations from the perfect law and consequently need an atonement.

Not only sin properly so called (that is, a voluntary transgression of a known law) but sin improperly so called (that is, an involuntary transgression of a divine law, known or unknown), needs the atoning blood.

Faith in Christ

Faith in Christ is not barely a speculative, rational thing, a cold, lifeless assent, a train of ideas in the head; but also a disposition of the heart.

And herein does it differ from that faith which the apostles themselves had while our Lord was on earth, that it acknowledges the necessity and merit of his death, and the power of his resurrection. It acknowledges his death as the only sufficient means of redeeming man from death eternal, and his resurrection as the restoration of us all to life and immortality; inasmuch as he 'was delivered for our sins, and rose again for our justification'.

Christian faith is, then, not only an assent to the whole gospel of Christ, but also a full reliance on the blood of Christ; a trust in the merits of his life, death and resurrection; a recumbency on him as our atonement and our life, as given for us, and living in us.

It is a sure confidence which a man hath in God, that through the merits of Christ, *his* sins are forgiven, and *he* is reconciled to the favour of God; and, in consequence hereof, a closing with him, and cleaving to him, as our 'wisdom, righteousness, sanctification and redemption', or, in one word, our salvation.

Believing the gospel

The gospel (that is, good tidings, good news for guilty, helpless sinners), in the largest sense of the word means the whole revelation made to men by Jesus Christ; and sometimes the whole account of what our Lord did and suffered while he tabernacled among men.

The substance of all is, 'Jesus Christ came into the world to save sinners'; or, 'God so loved the world that he gave his only-begotten Son, to the end that we might not perish, but have everlasting life'; or, 'He was wounded for our transgressions, he was bruised for our iniquities: the chastisement of our peace was upon him; and with his stripes we are healed.'

Believe this, and the Kingdom of God is thine. By faith thou attainest the promise: 'He pardoneth and absolveth all that truly repent, and unfeignedly believe his holy gospel.' As soon as ever God hath spoken to thy heart, 'Be of good cheer, thy sins are forgiven thee', his Kingdom comes: thou hast 'righteousness, and peace, and joy in the Holy Ghost'.

Justification by faith

What is it to be justified? It is not the being made actually just and righteous. This is sanctification; which is indeed, in some degree, the immediate fruit of justification but, nevertheless, is a distinct gift of God, and of a totally different nature. The one implies what God does for us through his Son; the other what he works in us by his Spirit.

Neither is that far-fetched conceit, that justification is the clearing us from accusation, particularly that of Satan, easily provable from any clear text of holy writ. It is also far easier to take for granted, than to prove from any clear scripture testimony, that justification is the clearing us from the accusation brought against us by the law.

Least of all does justification imply that God is deceived in those whom he justifies; that he thinks them to be what in fact they are not; that he accounts them to be otherwise than they are.

The plain scriptural notion of justification is pardon, the forgiveness of sins. It is that act of God the Father whereby, for the sake of the propitiation made by the blood of his Son, he 'showeth forth his righteousness' (or mercy) 'by the remission of sins that are past'.

The nature of salvation

This great gift of God, the salvation of our souls, which is begun on earth, but perfected in heaven, is no other than the image of God fresh stamped upon our hearts. It is a renewal in the spirit of our minds after the likeness of him that created us. It is a salvation from sin, and doubt and fear.

From fear; for, 'being justified freely', they who believe 'have peace with God through Jesus Christ our Lord, and rejoice in hope of the glory of God'. From doubt; for 'the Spirit of God beareth witness with their spirit, that they are the children of God'. And from sin; for 'being now made free from sin, they are servants of righteousness'.

God hath now 'laid the axe to the root of the tree, purifying their hearts by faith, and cleansing all the thoughts of their hearts by the inspiration of his Holy Spirit'. Having this hope, that they shall soon see God as he is, they 'purify themselves as he is pure', and are 'holy as he which hath called them is holy in all manner of conversation'.

Not that they have 'already attained' all they shall attain, neither are 'already', in this sense, 'perfect'. But they daily go on 'from strength to strength'. 'Beholding now as in a glass the glory of the Lord, they are changed into the same image, from glory to glory, as by the Spirit of the Lord'.

Grace and salvation

Salvation begins with what is usually termed (and very properly) *preventing grace*; including the first wish to please God, the first dawn of light concerning his will, and the first slight transient conviction of having sinned against him. All these imply some tendency towards life; some degree of salvation; the beginning of a deliverance from a blind, unfeeling heart, quite insensible of God and the things of God.

Salvation is carried on by *convincing grace*, usually in Scripture termed repentance; which brings a larger measure of self-knowledge and a further deliverance from the heart of stone.

Afterwards we experience the proper Christian salvation whereby 'through grace' we 'are saved by faith'; consisting of those two grand branches, justification and sanctification. By justification we are saved from the guilt of sin, and restored to the favour of God. By sanctification we are saved from the power and root of sin, and restored to the image of God.

Free grace

All the blessings which God hath bestowed upon man are of his mere grace, bounty, or favour; his free, undeserved favour; favour altogether undeserved, man having no claim to the least of his mercies.

It was free grace that 'formed man of the dust of the ground, and breathed into him a living soul', and stamped on that soul the image of God, and 'put all things under his feet'.

The same free grace continues to us at this day, life, and breath, and all things. For there is nothing we are, or have, or do, which can deserve the least thing at God's hand. 'All our works thou, O God, hast wrought in us.' These, therefore, are so many more instances of free mercy: and whatever righteousness may be found in man, this is also the gift of God.

Wherewithal then shall a sinful man atone for any the least of his sins? With his own works? No. Were they ever so many or holy, they are not his own, but God's. But indeed they are all unholy and sinful themselves, so that every one of them needs a fresh atonement.

Only corrupt fruit grows on a corrupt tree. And his heart is altogether corrupt and abominable, being 'come short of the glory of God', the glorious righteousness at first impressed on his soul, after the image of his great Creator. Therefore, having nothing, neither righteousness nor works, to plead, his mouth is utterly stopped before God.

If, then, sinful men find favour with God, it is 'grace upon grace'. If God vouchsafe still to pour fresh blessings upon us, yea, the greatest of all blessings, salvation; what can we say to these things but, 'Thanks be unto God for his unspeakable gift!'

And thus it is. Herein 'God commendeth his love towards us in that, while we were yet sinners, Christ died' to save us. 'By grace', then, 'are you saved through faith.' Grace is the source, faith the condition of salvation.

Responding to God's favour

When we have received any favour from God, we ought to retire, if not into our closets then into our hearts, and say, 'I come, Lord, to restore to thee what thou hast given, and I freely relinquish it, to enter again into my own nothingness.

'For what is the most perfect creature in heaven or earth in thy presence, but a void capable of being filled with thee and by thee: as the air which is void and dark is capable of being filled with the light of the sun, who withdraws it every day to restore it the next, there being nothing in the air that either appropriates this light or resists it?

'O give me the same facility of receiving and restoring thy grace and good works! I say, *thine*; for I acknowledge the root from which they spring is in thee, and not in me.'

No condemnation

Since a believer need not come into condemnation, even though he be *surprised* into what his soul abhors (suppose his being surprised is not owing to any carelessness or wilful neglect of his own); if thou who believest art thus overtaken in a fault, then grieve unto the Lord: it shall be a precious balm.

Pour out thy heart before him, and show him of thy trouble; and pray with all thy might to him who is 'touched with the feeling of thy infirmities', that he would establish, and strengthen, and settle thy soul, and suffer thee to fall no more.

But still he condemneth thee not. Wherefore shouldst thou fear? Thou hast no need of any 'fear that hath torment'. Thou shalt love him that loveth thee, and it sufficeth: more love will bring more strength. And as soon as thou lovest him with all thy heart, thou shalt be 'perfect and entire, lacking nothing'.

Wait in peace for that hour when 'the God of peace shall sanctify thee wholly, so that thy whole spirit and soul and body may be preserved blameless unto the coming of our Lord Jesus Christ'.

The necessity of the Spirit

As all merit is in the Son of God, in what he has done and suffered for us, so all power is in the Spirit of God. And therefore every man, in order to believe unto salvation, must receive the Holy Ghost. This is essentially necessary to every Christian, not in order to his working miracles, but in order to faith, peace, joy and love – the ordinary fruits of the Spirit.

Although no man on earth can explain the particular manner wherein the Spirit of God works on the soul, yet whosoever has these fruits cannot but know and *feel* that God has wrought them in his heart.

Sometimes he acts more particularly on the understanding, opening or enlightening it (as the Scripture speaks), and revealing, unveiling, discovering to us 'the deep things of God'.

Sometimes he acts on the wills and affections of men; withdrawing them from evil, inclining them to good, inspiring (breathing, as it were) good thoughts into them. So it has frequently been expressed, by an easy, natural metaphor, strictly analogous to *ruach, pneuma, spiritus*, and the words used in most modern tongues also, to denote the third person in the ever-blessed Trinity.

But however it be expressed, it is certain all true faith, and the whole work of salvation, every good thought, word, and work, is altogether by the operation of the Spirit of God.

The operations of the Spirit

Many years ago, when one was describing the glorious privilege of a believer, I cried out, 'If this be so, I have no faith'. He replied, 'You have faith, but it is weak'. The very same thing I say to you, my dear friend. You have faith, but it is only as a grain of mustard-seed. Hold fast what you have, and ask for what you want.

There is an irreconcilable variability in the operations of the Holy Spirit on the souls of men, more especially as to the manner of justification. Many find him rushing upon them like a torrent, while they experience 'the o'erwhelming power of saving grace'. This has been the experience of many.

But in others he works in a very different way:

'He deigns his influence to infuse,
  Sweet, refreshing, as the silent dews.'

It has pleased him to work the latter way in you from the beginning, and it is not improbable he will continue (as he has begun) to work in a gentle and almost insensible manner.

Let him take his own way. He is wiser than you; he will do all things well. Do not reason against him, but let the prayer of your heart be,

'Mould as thou wilt thy passive clay.'

Spiritual respiration

God is continually breathing, as it were, upon the soul; and his soul is breathing unto God. Grace is descending into his heart, and prayer and praise ascending to heaven: and by this intercourse between God and man, this fellowship with the Father and the Son, as by a kind of spiritual respiration, the life of God in the soul is sustained; and the child of God grows up, till he comes to the 'full measure of the stature of Christ'.

From hence it manifestly appears what is the nature of the new birth. It is that great change which God works in the soul when he brings it into life, when he raises it from the death of sin to the life of righteousness.

It is the change wrought in the whole soul by the almighty Spirit of God when it is 'created anew in Christ Jesus'; when it is 'renewed after the image of God in righteousness and true holiness'; when the love of the world is changed into the love of God; pride into humility; passion into meekness; hatred, envy, malice, into a sincere, tender, disinterested love for all mankind.

In a word, it is that change whereby the earthly, sensual, devilish mind is turned into the 'mind which was in Christ Jesus'. This is the nature of the new birth: 'So is every one that is born of the Spirit.'

The fruit of the Spirit

Let none ever presume to rest in any supposed testimony of the Spirit which is separate from the fruit of it. If the Spirit of God does really testify that we are the children of God, the immediate consequence will be the fruit of the Spirit, even 'love, joy, peace, long-suffering, gentleness, goodness, fidelity, meekness, temperance'.

And however this fruit may be clouded for a while during the time of strong temptation, so that it does not appear to the tempted person, while Satan is sifting him as wheat; yet the substantial part of it remains, even under the thickest cloud.

It is true, joy in the Holy Ghost may be withdrawn during the hour of trial; yea, the soul may be 'exceeding sorrowful' while 'the hour and power of darkness' continue; but even this is generally restored with increase, till we rejoice 'with joy unspeakable and full of glory'.

Let none rest in any supposed fruit of the Spirit without the witness. When we have once received this Spirit of adoption, this 'peace which passeth all understanding' will 'keep our hearts and minds in Christ Jesus'. And when this has brought forth its genuine fruit, all inward and outward holiness, it is undoubtedly the will of him that calleth us to give us always what he has once given.

The witness of our own spirit

Now this is properly the testimony of our own spirit; even the testimony of our own conscience, that God hath given us to be holy of heart, and holy in outward conversation. It is a consciousness of our having received, in and by the Spirit of adoption, the tempers mentioned in the Word of God as belonging to his adopted children; even a loving heart towards God, and towards all mankind; hanging with child-like confidence on God our Father, desiring nothing but him, casting all our care upon him, and embracing every child of man with earnest, tender affection, so as to be ready to lay down our life for our brother, as Christ laid down his life for us; a consciousness that we are inwardly conformed, by the Spirit of God, to the image of his Son, and that we walk before him in justice, mercy and truth, doing those things which are pleasing in his sight.

The witness of God's spirit

What is that testimony of God's Spirit, which is superadded to, and conjoined with this? How does he 'bear witness with our spirit that we are the children of God'? It is hard to find words in the language of men to explain 'the deep things of God'. Indeed, there are none that will adequately express what the children of God experience.

But perhaps one might say (desiring any that are taught of God to correct, to soften, or strengthen the expression), the testimony of the Spirit is an inward impression on the soul, whereby the Spirit of God directly witnesses to my spirit, that I am a child of God; that Jesus Christ hath loved me, and given himself for me; and that all my sins are blotted out, and I, even I, am reconciled to God.

That this testimony of the Spirit of God must needs, in the very nature of things, be antecedent to the testimony of our own spirit, may appear from this single consideration. We must love God, before we can be holy at all; this being the root of all holiness. Now we cannot love God, till we know he loves us. And we cannot know his pardoning love to us, till his Spirit witnesses it to our spirit.

A child of God

This it is, in the judgement of the Spirit of God, to be a son or a child of God; it is, so to *believe* in God, through Christ, as 'not to commit sin', and to enjoy at all times, and in all places, that 'peace of God which passeth all understanding'.

It is, so to *hope* in God through the Son of his love, as to have not only the 'testimony of a good conscience', but also the Spirit of God 'bearing witness with your spirits, that you are the children of God'; whence cannot but spring the rejoicing evermore in him through whom you 'have received the atonement'.

It is, so to *love* God who hath thus loved you, as you never did love any creature: so that you are constrained to love all men as yourselves with a love not only ever burning in your hearts, but flaming out in all your actions and conversations, and making your whole life one 'labour of love', one continued obedience to those commands, 'Be you merciful, as God is merciful'; 'Be you holy, as I the Lord am holy'; 'Be you perfect, as your Father which is in heaven is perfect.'

The thankful heart

He who hath this hope [in Christ], thus 'full of immortality, in everything giveth thanks' as knowing that this (whatsoever it is) 'is the will of God in Christ Jesus concerning him'. From him, therefore, he cheerfully receives all, saying, 'Good is the will of the Lord', and whether the Lord giveth or taketh away, equally 'blessing the name of the Lord'. For he hath 'learned in whatsoever state he is, therewith to be content'.

Whether in ease or pain, whether in sickness or health, whether in life or death, he giveth thanks from the ground of his heart to him who orders it for good; knowing that, as 'every good gift cometh from above', so none but good can come from the Father of lights, into whose hand he has wholly committed his body and soul as into the hands of a faithful Creator.

He is therefore 'careful' [anxious or uneasy] 'for nothing', as having 'cast all his care on him that careth for him' and 'in all things' resting on him, after 'making his request known to him with thanksgiving'.

The work of patience

What may we understand by the work of patience? 'Let patience have its perfect work.' It seems to mean, let it have its full fruit or effect. And what is the fruit which the Spirit of God is accustomed to produce hereby, in the heart of a believer? One immediate fruit of patience is peace: a sweet tranquillity of mind, a serenity of spirit, which can never be found unless where patience reigns.

And this peace often rises into joy. Even in the midst of various temptations, those that are enabled 'in patience to possess their souls' can witness not only quietness of spirit, but triumph and exultation.

Christian zeal is likewise confirmed and increased by patience, and so is activity in every good work, the same Spirit inciting us to be 'patient in bearing ill, and doing well'; making us equally willing to do and suffer the whole will of God.

But what is the *perfect* work of patience? Is it anything less than 'the perfect love of God' constraining us to love every soul of man, 'even as Christ loved us'?

A catholic spirit

A man of a catholic spirit is one who gives his hand to all whose hearts are right with his heart: one who knows how to value, and praise God for, all the advantages he enjoys with regard to the knowledge of the things of God, the true scriptural manner of worshipping him and, above all, his union with a congregation fearing God and working righteousness: one who, retaining these blessings with the strictest care, keeping them as the apple of his eye, at the same time loves all, of whatever opinion or worship, or congregation, who believe in the Lord Jesus Christ; who love God and man; who, rejoicing to please and fearing to offend God, are careful to abstain from evil and zealous of good works.

He is the man of a truly catholic spirit who bears all these continually upon his heart; who, having an unspeakable tenderness for their persons, and longing for their welfare, does not cease to commend them to God in prayer, as well as to plead their cause before men; who speaks comfortably to them and labours, by all his words, to strengthen their hands in God. He assists them to the uttermost of his power in all things, spiritual and temporal. He is ready 'to spend and be spent for them'; yea, to lay down his life for their sake.

An inward heaven

As our knowledge and our love of God increase, by the same degree and in the same proportion the kingdom of an inward heaven must necessarily increase also, while we 'grow up in all things into him who is our head'.

And when we are 'complete in him', as our translators render it, but more properly when we are 'filled with him'; when 'Christ in us, the hope of glory' is our God and our all; when he has taken the full possession of our heart; when he reigns therein without a rival, the Lord of every motion there; when we dwell in Christ and Christ in us, we are one with Christ and Christ with us: then we are completely happy, then we live 'all the life that is hid with Christ in God', then, and not until then, we properly experience what that word meaneth, 'God is love; and whosoever dwelleth in love, dwelleth in God and God in him.'

Love, the highest gift

Love is the highest gift of God; humble, gentle, patient love. All visions, revelations, manifestations whatever are little things compared to love.

It were well you should be thoroughly sensible of this – the heaven of heavens is love. There is nothing higher in religion; there is, in effect, nothing else. If you look for anything but more love, you are looking wide of the mark, you are getting out of the royal way.

And when you are asking others, 'Have you received this or that blessing?' if you mean anything but more love, you mean wrongly. You are leading them out of the way, and putting them upon a false scent.

Settle it, then, in your heart that from the moment God has saved you from all sin, you are to aim at nothing more but more of that love described in the thirteenth chapter of Corinthians. You can go no higher than this until you are carried into Abraham's bosom.

Love to all

Seeing thou canst do all things through Christ strengthening thee, be merciful as thy Father in heaven is merciful. Love thy neighbour as thyself. Love friends and enemies as thine own soul; and let thy love be long-suffering and patient towards all men.

Let it be kind, soft, benign; inspiring thee with the most amiable sweetness, and the most fervent and tender affection. Let it rejoice in the truth wheresoever it is found; the truth that is after godliness. Enjoy whatever brings glory to God, and promotes peace and goodwill among men.

In love, cover all things. Of the dead and the absent speak nothing but good. Believe all things which may in any way tend to clear your neighbour's character. Hope all things in his favour and endure all things, triumphing over all opposition: for true love never faileth, in time or in eternity.

The Kingdom of God

'The Kingdom of God', saith our blessed Lord, 'is within you.' It is no outward, no distant thing; but 'a well of living water' in the soul, 'springing up into everlasting life'. It is 'righteousness, and peace, and joy in the Holy Ghost'. It is holiness and happiness.

The general manner in which it pleases God to set it up in the heart is this. A sinner, being drawn by the love of the Father, enlightened by the Son ('the true light who lighteth every man that cometh into the world') and convinced of sin by the Holy Ghost; through the preventing grace which is given him freely, cometh weary and heavy-laden, and casteth all his sins upon him that is 'mighty to save'.

He receiveth from him true, living faith. Being justified by faith, he hath peace with God. He rejoices in hope of the glory of God, and knows that sin has no more dominion over him. And the love of God is shed abroad in his heart, producing all holiness of heart and conversation.

The meaning of sanctification

At the same time that we are justified, yea, in that very moment, sanctification begins. In that instant we are born again, born from above, born of the Spirit: there is a *real* as well as a *relative* change. We are inwardly renewed by the power of God.

From the time of our being born again, the gradual work of sanctification takes place. We are enabled 'by the Spirit' to 'mortify the deeds of the body' of our evil nature; and as we are more and more dead to sin, we are more and more alive to God. We go on from grace to grace.

It is thus that we wait for entire sanctification; for a full salvation from all our sins – from pride, self-will, anger, unbelief; or, as the apostle expressed it, 'go on unto perfection'.

But what is perfection? The word has various senses. Here it means perfect love. It is love excluding sin; love filling the heart, taking up the whole capacity of the soul. It is love 'rejoicing evermore, praying without ceasing, in everything giving thanks'.

The ladder of perfection

This is the fulfilling of the law, the last stage of Christian holiness. This maketh the man of God perfect. He that being dead to the world is alive to God; the desire of whose soul is unto his name; who has given him his whole heart; who delights in him, and in nothing else but what tends to him; who, for his sake, burns with love to all mankind; who neither thinks, speaks, nor acts but to fulfil his will – is on the last round of the ladder to heaven. Grace hath had its full work upon his soul. The next step he takes is into glory.

May the God of glory give unto us who have not already attained to this, neither are already perfect, to do this one thing: forgetting those things which are behind, and reaching forth unto those things which are before, to press towards the mark for the prize of our high calling in Christ Jesus!

May he so enlighten our eyes that we may reckon all things but loss for the excellency of the knowledge of Christ Jesus our Lord; and so establish our hearts that we may rejoice to suffer the loss of all things and count them but dung that we may win Christ!

A perfect man

We understand by that scriptural expression, 'a perfect man', one in whom God hath fulfilled his faithful word: 'From all your filthiness, and from all your idols, will I cleanse you. I will also save you from all your uncleannesses.' We understand hereby one whom God hath sanctified throughout, even in body, soul and spirit; one who walketh in the light, as he is in the light; in whom there is no darkness at all; the blood of Jesus Christ his Son having cleansed him from all sin.

He loveth the Lord his God with all his heart and serveth him with all his strength. He loveth his neighbour (every man) as himself; yea, as Christ loved us: those in particular who despitefully use him and persecute him because they know not the Son, neither the Father. Indeed, his soul is all love.

And his life agreeth thereto; full of 'the work of faith, the patience of hope, the labour of love'. And whatsoever he doeth, either in word or deed, he doeth it all in the name, in the love and power, of the Lord Jesus. In a word, he doeth the will of God on earth as it is done in heaven.

Sin in believers

This grand point, that there are two contrary principles in believers – nature and grace, the flesh and the spirit – runs through all the Epistles of St Paul, yea, through all the Holy Scriptures; almost all the directions and exhortations therein are founded on this supposition; pointing at wrong tempers or practices in those who are, notwithstanding, acknowledged by the inspired writers to be believers. And they are continually exhorted to fight with and conquer these by the power of the faith which was in them.

'But can Christ be in the same heart where sin is?' Undoubtedly he can; otherwise it could never be saved therefrom. Where the sickness is, there is the Physician,

> 'Carrying on his work within,
> Striving till he cast out sin.'

Christ indeed cannot *reign* where sin *reigns*; neither will he *dwell* where any sin is *allowed*. But he *is* and *dwells* in the heart of every believer who is *fighting against* all sin; although it be not yet purified according to the purification of the sanctuary.

Sins of omission

Beware of sins of omission. Lose no opportunity of doing good in any kind. Be zealous of good works. Willingly omit no work, either of piety or mercy. Do all the good you possibly can to the bodies and souls of men. Particularly, 'thou shalt in anywise reprove thy neighbour, and not suffer sin upon him'.

Be active. Give no place to indolence or sloth. Give no occasion to say, 'You are idle, you are idle.' Many will say so still, but let your whole spirit and behaviour refute the slander. Be always employed; lose no shred of time; gather up the fragments, that nothing be lost. And whatsoever thy hand findeth to do, do it with thy might.

Be 'slow to speak', and wary in speaking. 'In a multitude of words there wanteth not sin.' Do not talk much, neither long at a time. Few can converse profitably above an hour. Keep at the utmost distance from pious chit-chat, from religious gossiping.

Perpetual vigilance

If, after having renounced all, we do not watch incessantly, and beseech God to accompany our vigilance with his, we shall be again entangled and overcome.

As the most dangerous winds may enter at little openings, so the devil never enters more dangerously than by little, unobserved incidents which seem to be nothing, yet insensibly open the heart to great temptations.

It is good to renew ourselves, from time to time, by closely examining the state of our souls, as if we had never done it before; for nothing tends more to the full assurance of faith than to keep ourselves by this means in humility, and the exercise of all good works.

To continual watchfulness and prayer ought to be added continual employment. For grace flies a vacuum as well as nature, and the devil fills whatever God does not fill.

There is no faithfulness like that which ought to be between a guide of souls and the person directed by him. They ought continually to regard each other in God, and closely to examine themselves, whether all their thoughts are pure and all their words directed with Christian discretion. Other affairs are only the things of men, but these are peculiarly the things of God.

Dealing with temptation

You must now expect temptations. Perhaps they will assault you on every side, for all the powers of hell are enraged at you and will use every art to move you from your steadfastness. But he that is for you is greater than all that are against you: only beware of evil reasoning!

Hang simply on him that loves you, and whom you love; just as a helpless little child. Christ is yours, all yours: that is enough. Lean your whole soul upon him! You never need lose anything that God has given, so you keep close to him.

As soon as you had your armour on, it was fit that you should be proved; so God prepared for you the occasions of fighting, that you might conquer and might know both your own weakness and his strength. Each day will bring just temptation enough and power enough to conquer it.

Spiritual heaviness

How wide is the difference between darkness of soul and heaviness; which, nevertheless, are so generally confounded with each other, even by experienced Christians. Darkness, or the wilderness state, implies a total loss of joy in the Holy Ghost. Heaviness does not: in the midst of this we may 'rejoice with joy unspeakable'.

They that are in darkness have lost the peace of God. They that are in heaviness have not: so far from it that at the very time 'peace' as well as 'grace' may 'be multiplied' unto them. In the former, the love of God is waxed cold, if it be not utterly extinguished. In the latter, it retains its full force or, rather, increases daily.

In these faith itself, if not totally lost, is, however, grievously decayed. Those, though they see him not, yet have a clear, unshaken confidence in God, and an abiding evidence of that love whereby all their sins are blotted out.

Self-denial

What is self-denial? Wherein are we to deny ourselves? And whence does the necessity of this arise? I answer, the will of God is the supreme, unalterable rule for every intelligent creature, equally binding every angel in heaven and every man upon earth. Nor can it be otherwise: this is the natural, necessary result of the relation between creatures and their Creator.

But if the will of God be our one rule of action in everything, great and small, it follows, by undeniable consequence, that we are not to do our own will in anything. Here, therefore, we see at once the nature, with the ground and reason, of self-denial.

We see the nature of self-denial: it is the denying or refusing to follow our own will, from a conviction that the will of God is the only rule of action to us. And we see the reason thereof, because we are creatures; because 'it is he that hath made us, and not we ourselves'.

True resignation

We ought quietly to suffer whatever befalls us, to bear the defects of others and our own, to confess them to God in secret prayer, or with groans which cannot be uttered; but never to speak a sharp or peevish word, nor to murmur or repine.

We are to bear with those we cannot amend and to be content with offering them to God. This is true resignation. And since he has borne our infirmities, we may well bear those of each other for his sake.

To abandon all, to strip one's self of all, in order to seek and to follow Jesus Christ naked to Bethlehem, where he was born: naked to the hall where he was scourged: and naked to Calvary where he died on the cross, is so great a mercy that neither the thing nor the knowledge of it is given to any but through faith in the Son of God.

The snare of pride

Watch and pray continually against pride. If God has cast it out, see that it enter no more. It is fully as dangerous as desire. And you may slide back into it unawares, especially if you think there is no danger of it. 'Nay, but I ascribe all I have to God.' So you may, and be proud nevertheless. For it is pride, not only to ascribe anything we have to ourselves, but to think we have what we really have not.

If you think you have more than you really have; or if you think you are so taught of God as no longer to need man's teaching, pride lieth at the door. Do not therefore say to any who would advise or reprove you, 'You are blind; you cannot teach me.' Do not say, 'This is your wisdom, your carnal reason'; but calmly weigh the thing before God.

Always remember, much grace does not imply much light. These do not always go together. As there may be much light where there is but little love, so there may be much love where there is little light.

Clothed with humility

Suppose God has now thoroughly cleansed our heart and scattered the last remains of sin; yet how can we be sensible enough of our own helplessness, our utter inability to all good, unless we are every hour, yea, every moment, 'endued with power from on high'?

We have need, even in this state of grace, to be thoroughly and continually penetrated with a sense of this. Otherwise we shall be in perpetual danger of robbing God of his honour by glorying in something we have received as though we had not received it.

When our inmost soul is thoroughly tinctured therewith, it remains that we be 'clothed with humility'. The word used by St Peter seems to imply that we be covered with it as with a surtout;* that we be all humility, both within and without; tincturing all we think, speak and do.

Let all our actions spring from this fountain; let all our words breathe this spirit; that all men may know we have been with Jesus and have learned of him to be lowly in heart.

* Overcoat

The lowly mind

Let there 'be in you that lowly mind which was in Christ Jesus'. Let modesty and self-diffidence appear in all your words and actions. Let all you speak and do show that you are little, and base, and mean, and vile in your own eyes.

As one instance of this, be always ready to own any fault you have been in. If you have at any time thought, spoken, or acted wrongly, be not backward to acknowledge it. Never dream that this will hurt the cause of God; no, it will further it. Be therefore open and frank, when you are taxed with anything. Do not seek either to evade or disguise it, but let it appear just as it is, and you will thereby not hinder but adorn the gospel.

The knowledge of ourselves is true humility; and without this we cannot be free from vanity, a desire of praise being inseparably connected with every degree of pride. Continual watchfulness is absolutely necessary to hide this from stealing in upon us. But as long as we steadily watch and pray, we shall not enter into temptation. It may and will assault us on every side, but it cannot prevail.

The obedient believer

His one desire is the one design of his life, namely, 'not to do his own will, but the will of him that sent him'. His one intention at all times and in all things is, not to please himself, but him whom his soul loveth. He has a single eye. And because 'his eye is single, his whole body is full of light'.

God then reigns alone. All that is in the soul is holiness to the Lord. There is not a motion in his heart but is according to his will. Every thought that arises points to him, and is in obedience to the law of Christ.

And the tree is known by its fruits. For as he loves God, so he keeps his commandments; not only some, or most of them, but all, from the least to the greatest. He is not content to 'keep the whole law, and offend in one point', but has, in all points, 'a conscience void of offence towards God and towards man'.

Whatever God has forbidden, he avoids; whatever God hath enjoined, he doeth; and that whether it be little or great, hard or easy, joyous or grievous to the flesh. All the commandments of God he accordingly keeps, and that with all his might. For his obedience is in proportion to his love, the source from whence it flows.

The praying believer

He 'prays without ceasing'. It is given him 'always to pray, and not to faint'. Not that he is always in the house of prayer, though he neglects no opportunity of being there. Neither is he always on his knees, although he often is, or on his face, before the Lord his God. Nor yet is he always crying aloud to God, or calling upon him in words. For many times 'the Spirit maketh intercession for him with groans that cannot be uttered'.

But at all times the language of his heart is this: 'Thou brightness of the eternal glory, unto thee is my heart, though without a voice, and my silence speaketh unto thee.' And this is true prayer, and this alone. But his heart is ever lifted up to God, at all times and in all places.

In this he is never hindered, much less interrupted, by any person or thing. In retirement or company, in leisure, business, or conversation, his heart is ever with the Lord. Whether he lie down or rise up, God is in all his thoughts. He walks with God continually, having the loving eye of his mind still fixed upon him, and everywhere 'seeing him that is invisible'.

Continual prayer

God's command to 'pray without ceasing' is founded on the necessity we have of his grace to preserve the life of God in the soul, which can no more subsist one moment without it than the body can without air.

Whether we think of or speak to God, whether we act or suffer for him, all is prayer when we have no other object than his love and the desire of pleasing him.

All that a Christian does, even in eating and sleeping, is prayer when it is done in simplicity according to the order of God, without either adding to or diminishing it by his own choice.

Prayer continues in the desire of the heart, though the understanding be employed on outward things. In souls filled with love the desire to please God is a continual prayer.

Prayer as communion with God

A higher degree of that peace which may well be said to pass all understanding will keep, not only your heart, but all the workings of your mind (as the word properly signifies), both of your reason and imagination, from all irregular sallies. This peace will increase as your faith increases: one always keeps pace with the other. So that on this account also your continual prayer should be, 'Lord, increase my faith!'

A continual desire is a continual prayer – that is, in a low sense of the word; for there is a far higher sense, such an open intercourse with God, such a close, uninterrupted communion with him, as Gregory Lopez* experienced, and not a few of our brethren and sisters now alive. One of them (a daughter of sorrow for a long time) was talking with me this morning. This you also should aspire after; as you know, he with whom we have to do is no respecter of persons.

* Gregory Lopez (1611–87) was a Dominican who became the first native Chinese bishop.

Ask, seek, knock

O how meek and gentle, how lowly in heart, how full of love both to God and man, might you have been at this day, if you had only asked – if you had continued instant in prayer! Therefore now, at least, 'ask, and it shall be given unto you'.

Ask that you may thoroughly experience and perfectly practise the whole of that religion which our Lord has here so beautifully described. It shall then be given you to be holy as he is holy, both in heart and in all manner of conversation.

Seek, in the way he hath ordained, in searching the Scriptures, in hearing his word, in meditating thereon, in fasting, in partaking of the Supper of the Lord, and surely you shall find. You shall find that pearl of great price, that faith which overcometh the world, that peace which the world cannot give, that love which is the earnest of your inheritance.

Knock: continue in prayer, and in every other way of the Lord. Be not weary or faint in your mind. Press on to the mark. Take no denial. Let him not go, until he bless you. 'And the door' of mercy, of holiness, of heaven 'shall be opened unto you.'

On fasting

I am to show in what manner we are to fast, that it may be an acceptable service unto the Lord. And, first, let it be done unto the Lord, with our eye singly fixed on him. Let our intention herein be this, and this alone, to glorify our Father which is in heaven. Let us beware of mocking God, of turning our fast, as well as our prayers, into an abomination unto the Lord, by the mixture of any temporal view, particularly by seeking the praise of men.

Let us beware, secondly, of fancying that we *merit* anything of God by our fasting. We cannot be too often warned of this, inasmuch as a desire to 'establish our own righteousness', to procure salvation of debt and not of grace, is so deeply rooted in all our hearts. Fasting is only a way which God hath ordained, wherein we wait for his unmerited mercy, and wherein, without any desert of ours, he hath promised freely to give us his blessing.

Not that we are to imagine that performing the bare outward act will receive any blessing from God. Let us take care to afflict our souls as well as our bodies. Let every season, either of public or private fasting, be a season of exercising all those holy affections which are implied in a broken and contrite heart.

Preparing for Communion

In order to understand the nature of the Lord's Supper it would be useful carefully to read over those passages in the Gospel and in the First Epistle to the Corinthians which speak of the institution of it. Hence we learn that the design of this sacrament is the continual remembrance of the death of Christ, by eating bread and drinking wine which are the outward signs of the inward grace, the Body and Blood of Christ.

It is highly expedient for those who purpose to receive this, whenever their time will permit, to prepare themselves for this solemn ordinance by self-examination and prayer. But this is not absolutely necessary. And when we have not time for it, we should see that we have the habitual preparation which is absolutely necessary and can never be dispensed with on any account or any occasion whatever. This is, first, a full *purpose* of heart to keep all the commandments of God; and, secondly, a sincere *desire* to receive all his promises.

The pilgrim's guidebook

I am a creature of a day, passing through life as an arrow through the air. I am a spirit come from God, and returning to God; just hovering over the great gulf until, a few moments hence, I am no more seen. I drop into an unchangeable eternity!

I want to know one thing – the way to heaven; how to land safe on that happy shore. God himself has condescended to teach the way; for this very end he came from heaven. He hath written it down in a book.

O give me that book! At any price, give me the book of God! I have it: here is knowledge enough for me.

Using the Bible

Here then I am, far from the busy ways of men.
I sit down alone: only God is here. In his presence
I open, I read his book; for this end, to find the
way to heaven. Is there a doubt concerning the
meaning of what I read? Does anything appear
dark or intricate?

I lift up my heart to the Father of lights: 'Lord, is
it not thy word, "If any man lack wisdom, let
him ask of God"? Thou "givest liberally, and
upbraidest not". Thou hast said, "If any be willing
to do thy will, he shall know." I am willing to
do, let me know thy will.'

I then search after and consider parallel passages
of Scripture, 'comparing spiritual things with
spiritual'. I meditate thereon with all the attention
and earnestness of which my mind is capable. If
any doubt still remains, I consult those who are
experienced in the things of God, and then the
writings whereby they, being dead, yet speak.

The Christian rule

The Christian rule of right and wrong is the word of God, the writings of the Old and New Testaments; all that the prophets and 'holy men of old' wrote 'as they were moved by the Holy Ghost'; all that Scripture which was 'given by inspiration of God' and which is indeed 'profitable for doctrine', or teaching the whole will of God; 'for reproof' of what is contrary thereto; for 'correction' of error; and 'for instruction', or training us up, 'in righteousness'.

This is a lantern unto a Christian's feet, and a light in all his paths. This alone he receives as his rule of right or wrong, of whatever is really good or evil. He esteems nothing good but what is here enjoined, either directly or by plain consequence; he accounts nothing evil but what is here forbidden, either in terms or by undeniable inference.

Whatever the Scripture neither forbids nor enjoins he believes to be of an indifferent nature, to be in itself neither good nor evil, this being the whole and sole outward rule whereby his conscience is to be directed in all things.

The role of reason

Let reason do all that reason can. Employ it as far as it will go. But, at the same time, acknowledge that it is utterly incapable of giving either faith, or hope, or love, and consequently of producing either real virtue or substantial happiness.

Expect these from a higher source, even from the Father of the spirits of all flesh. Seek and receive them, not as your own acquisition, but as the gift of God. Lift up your hearts to him who 'giveth to all men liberally and upbraideth not'.

He alone can give that faith which is 'the evidence' and conviction 'of things not seen'. He alone can 'beget you unto a lively hope' of an inheritance eternal in the heavens; and he alone can 'shed his love abroad in your heart by the Holy Ghost given unto you'.

Ask, therefore, and it shall be given you! Cry unto him, and you shall not cry in vain! So shall you be living witnesses that wisdom, holiness and happiness are one, are inseparably united and are indeed the beginning of that eternal life which God hath given us in his Son.

The peril of disunity

Beware of schism, of making a rent in the Church of Christ. That inward disunion, the members ceasing to have a reciprocal love 'one for another', is the very root of all contention and every outward separation. Beware of everything tending thereto. Beware of a dividing spirit: shun whatever has the least aspect that way.

Suffer not one thought of separating from your brethren, whether their opinion agrees with yours or not. Do not dream that any man sins in not believing you, in not taking your word; or that this or that opinion is essential to the work, and both must stand or fall together.

Beware of impatience with contradiction. Do not condemn or think hardly of those who cannot see just as you see, or who judge it their duty to contradict you, whether in a great thing or a small. I fear some of us have thought hardly of others merely because they contradicted what we affirmed. All this tends to division; and by everything of this kind, we are teaching them an evil lesson against ourselves.

O beware of touchiness, of testiness, not bearing to be spoken to; starting at the least word; and flying from those who do not implicitly receive mine or another's sayings!

Christian stewardship

You see the nature and extent of truly Christian prudence so far as it relates to the use of that great talent, money. Gain all you can, without hurting either yourself or your neighbour, in soul or body. Save all you can, by cutting off every expense which serves only to indulge foolish desire. Then give all you can or, in other words, give all you have to God.

I entreat you in the name of the Lord Jesus, act up to the dignity of your calling! No more sloth! Whatsoever your hand findeth to do, do it with your might. No more waste! Cut off every expense which fashion, caprice, or flesh and blood demand. No more covetousness! But employ whatever God has entrusted you with, in doing good, all possible good, in every possible kind and degree, to the household of faith, to all men. This is no small part of 'the wisdom of the just'.

Give all you have, as well as all you are, a spiritual sacrifice to him who withheld not from you his Son, his only Son: so 'laying up in store for yourselves a good foundation against the time to come, that you may attain eternal life'.

Suffering for Christ's sake

Expect contradiction and opposition, together with crosses of various kinds. Consider the words of St Paul: 'To you it is given, on behalf of Christ' – for his sake, as a fruit of his death and intercession for you – 'not only to believe, but also to suffer for his sake.'

It is given! God gives you this opposition or reproach; it is a fresh token of his love. And will you disown the Giver, or spurn his gift, and count it a misfortune? Will you not rather say, 'Father, the hour is come, that thou shouldst be glorified. Now thou givest thy child to suffer something for thee. Do with me according to thy will.'

Know that these things, far from being hindrances to the work of God, or to your soul, unless by your own fault, are not only unavoidable in the course of providence, but profitable, yea, necessary for you. Therefore receive them from God (not from chance) with willingness, with thankfulness. Receive them from men with humility, meekness, yieldingness, gentleness, sweetness.

Spiritual warfare

Let us, therefore, hold fast the sound doctrine 'once delivered to the saints', and delivered down by them, with the written word, to all succeeding generations: that, although we are renewed, cleansed, purified, sanctified, the moment we truly believe in Christ, yet we are not then renewed, cleansed, purified altogether; but the flesh, the evil nature, still *remains* (though subdued), and wars against the Spirit.

So much the more let us use all diligence in 'fighting the good fight of faith'. So much the more earnestly let us 'watch and pray' against the enemy within. The more carefully let us take to ourselves and 'put on the whole armour of God'; that, although 'we wrestle' both 'with flesh and blood, and with principalities, and powers, and wicked spirits in high places', we 'may be able to withstand in the evil day, and having done all, to stand'.

Light must shine

It is impossible for any that have it to conceal the religion of Jesus Christ. This our Lord makes plain beyond all contradiction by a twofold comparison: 'You are the light of the world: a city set upon a hill cannot be hid.'

You Christians are 'the light of the world' with regard both to your tempers and actions. Your holiness makes you as conspicuous as the sun in the midst of heaven. As you cannot go out of the world, so neither can you stay in it without appearing to all mankind. You may not flee from men; and while you are among them, it is impossible to hide your lowliness and meekness, and those other dispositions whereby you aspire to be perfect as your Father which is in heaven is perfect.

Love cannot be hid any more than light; and least of all when it shines forth in action when you exercise yourselves in the labour of love, in beneficence of every kind. As well may men think to hide a city as to hide a Christian; yea, as well may they conceal a city set upon a hill as a holy, zealous, active lover of God and man.

'Without holiness no man shall see the Lord', shall see the face of God in glory. Nothing under heaven can be more sure than this: 'For the mouth of the Lord hath spoken it. And though heaven and earth pass away, yet his word shall not pass away.' As well therefore might God fall from heaven, as his word fall to the ground.

No, it cannot be. None shall live with God but he that now lives to God. None shall enjoy the glory of God in heaven but he that bears the image of God on earth. None that is not saved from sin here can be saved from hell hereafter. None can see the Kingdom of God above unless the Kingdom of God be in him below.

Whosoever will reign with Christ in heaven must have Christ reigning in him on earth. He must have 'that mind in him which was in Christ', enabling him 'to walk as Christ also walked'.

Sources and Index

Although a new edition of John Wesley's writings is being prepared and several volumes have already appeared, the only completed collection remains that made by Thomas Jackson in the last century. It has been reprinted by Zondervan in the USA.

The standard edition of Wesley's Journal, edited by Nehemiah Curnock, was produced in eight volumes between 1909 and 1916, and that of his Letters, edited by John Telford, also in eight volumes, came out in 1931. Both sets were published by the Epworth Press, together with the two volumes of the Standard Sermons, edited by Edward H. Sugden (1921).

The Journal, Letters and Standard Sermons are all included in the *Works* assembled by Jackson, along with further sermons, treatises, appeals and tracts, but the more recent sources are listed below, when relevant, as being easily accessible. Although the Journal is quoted in the Introduction, no extract is included in the devotional selection. The sources are indicated as follows: *W* – *Works*; S – Standard Sermons; L – Letters. Volume and page numbers are added in each case. The first figure in bold type refers to a page of the present book.

The text stands substantially as it came from Wesley's pen, but the capitalization and punctuation have been pruned in places.

1	*W* 8:197–8	31	S 2:446–8
2	*W* 11:432	32	*W* 14:272
3	S 2:34	33	*W* 14:329–30
4	S 1:197–8	34	S 2:367–9
5	*W* 7:324–5	35	*W* 11: 432
6	S 2:233–4	36	*W* 11:439
7	*W* 11:395–6	37	L 5:94, 237
8	S 1:39–41	38	S 2:277–8
9	S 1:159	39	S 2:285–6
10	S 1:119–20	40	*W* 11:436–7
11	*W* 14:323–4	41	*W* 11:427–8
12	*W* 6:509	42	*W* 6:398
13	S 1:37	43	*W* 11:428; L 5:82
14	S 1:37–8	44	*W* 8:344
15	*W* 11:441	45	*W* 8:343
16	S 1:177	46	*W* 11:438
17	*W* 8:49	47	L 5:282–3
18	L 7:298	48	S 1:527–8
19	S 2:234	49	S 1:466–8
20	S 2:358–9	50	*W* 7:149
21	S 1:207	51	S 1:31–2
22	S 1:207–8	52	S 1:32
23	S 1:294	53	S 1:225–6
24	*W* 8:342–3	54	*W* 6:360
25	*W* 6:486–7	55	*W* 11:433–4
26	S 2:145–6	56	S 2:326–7
27	*W* 6:430–31	57	*W* 11:434
28	*W* 11:430	58	S 2:378
29	S 2:35–6	59	S 1:388–9
30	*W* 14:211–12	60	*W* 10:364